Organic Allotment Journal Planner

Planning and Planting your Allotment
Black and white version

Sue Messruther

First Printing, 2018

ISBN-13: 978-1727013689

ISBN-10: 1727013689

I dedicate this book to

Those who strive to grow and produce their own healthy and organic food.

All of the digging, turning, pruning and planting is so satisfying when you can sit and eat your own home grown produce, there is nothing more exciting than to show what you have grown or bringing a bag of goodies home from the allotment at the end of the day.

I always like to plant a few extras, some for the bugs and some for family and friends by sharing we are not only showing we care but we are sharing good health.

Contents

From the Author

This book is not designed to go into a lot of details about how to plant, etc. rather it offers ideas and tips that I have tried, this book has been in the making for a few years now as I experimented with different types of gardening and the results are, I do diverse organic gardening! Sometimes I do no dig and sometimes I dig, some are in raised beds, some are not − these are all in different sections of my allotment. I keep experimenting and trying new things, but always organic that is my hard-fast rule!

The idea for this book came about because I had my plans on scrap pieces of papers and my year to year bed planning was always not where I left it or I thought I had put it somewhere and wanted to refer back to it but couldn't place where I had put the paper! So, I scrapped that idea and decided I need a journal for my allotment!

And so now here it is, and I hope you find it as useful as I do.

Sue Messruther

CHAPTER ONE

Organic Gardening

Organic gardening is a system that avoids using chemicals such as pesticides and artificial fertilises, rather it relies on crop rotation, composting, animal manures, legumes, green manures and biological controls to keep the soil fertile and to manage pests, diseases and weed problems.

The soil is a living system that gardeners work with rather than attempt to dominate with powerful fertilisers and pesticides. Maintaining genetic diversity of crops by growing a large range of varieties while encouraging wildlife in and around the allotment, avoiding waste and pollution, recycling organic materials whenever possible.

The organic gardener approaches pests with items such as mesh and fleece rather than pesticides or companion planting. It is said that organic gardening is an all or nothing commitment and the good produces is superior to mass produced foods.

Allotment gardeners who go the organic approach need to realise that their neighbours may not have the same ideas. The biggest question most ask is where do you start?

You start with your soil or from the ground up if you will allow the pun! To prepare your organic allotment growing area, whether it is a single bed or a large allotment you start working with your soil and composting. It will aid you to produce the rich and nutrient bursting soil that will develop and feed your plants.

It's sensible to plan your planting, keeping notes of what veg will grow where. The wise and informed gardener can keep themselves in vegetables all year round, along with soil management of rotating where you plant your crops from year to year, to avoid disease and to make best use of your soil's productiveness.

A good organicc soil management is important if you want your plants to grow well. Healthy, fertile soil, with a good organic structure, which lets your plants absorb water and nutrients, and boosts strong growth. It is possibly the utmost important part of growing organically.

To feed the soil, and improve its structure, use organic materials like garden compost, rotted manures or leaf mould. All of these materials release nutrients gradually, while improving soil conditions, and provide the perfect conditions for vital microorganisms.

CHAPTER TWO

Digging Methods

Gardeners of old would dig down two or three spade depths, a very laborious method, but it actually paves the way for a no dig garden approach or raised beds.

To double or triple dig a trench is dug about 60cm/18 inches wide a spades depth deep. This base is then forked or dug over where manure or compost is added along the way. This stabilizes the soil and prolongs the benefits of digging for some years if the soil is not trampled or worked when wet. The next trench is then dug next to the one just dug, the soil from the second trench is rejuvenated with organic matter and fills the first trench and so forth until the beds are dug over.

Why do they double dig?

Double digging in trenches will increase the depth of the topsoil and produces better crops it is generally done when the soil is compacted or previously cultivated and is not necessary to double dig every year unless your soil is poor and heavy otherwise every 3 to 5 years is enough.

Double digging is used to increase soil drainage and aeration. This involves the loosening of two layers of soil, and the addition of organic matter. Double digging is characteristically done when cultivating soil in a new garden, or when deep topsoil is essential.

Generally done in autumn and winter because the ground is moist but not waterlogged or frozen and it gives time to settle down where the frosts will break down the lumpy clods you are left with before planting in spring

No dig

No dig beds involves growing crops in beds that can be reached from narrow paths of around 18 inches from either side and is never trodden on. The beds can be raised or flat and no dig regime the weeds are controlled by shallow hoeing or hand weeding then mulching.

Mulches also take place of "earthing up" potatoes. Because there is little disturbance of the soil, no weed seeds are brought to the surface and any that are already near the surface geminate then get pulled and mulched will decline another added benefit of the no dig garden is that the clods produced by digging reduces cover for slugs, a no dig garden is well worth trying particularly for those who are less able.

This method of cultivation requires a great deal of mulch (well-rotted manure or compost) and persistence. By not digging you will not be exposing the soil to weed seeds. As a result, the existing weeds are kept in darkness, and therefore causes them to weaken and die.

It is very easy create your no dig garden, all you have to do is apply very thick, well decomposed mulch over your beds and press it down well to make it firm, the worms will burrow their way up and munch away on the organic matter taking it back down to the soil creating a rich and well textured soil.

You then plant or sow seeds directly to the ground as you would normally do disturbing very little soil means there are less weeds to hoe, you can use a rake to prepare a soft crumbly tilth on the surface for the seeds. Using a trowel, you can easily remove any weeds that do appear, and you can expect them to appear for up to a year for the perennials, of course the annual weeds will die with a few months, unfortunately bindweed and marestail will survive but they will be weak and easily removed.

Then each year you replace the compost or manure in the autumn when the crops have finished or in spring for the winter crops. If you have a weed infested area and plenty of time, then cover it with thick cardboard, then heaps of manure and mulch over the top, it will take a year to mulch down and weaken the weeds, but then in spring you can make holes in it easily to plant your vegetables while you are waiting for the weeds to die off.

Raised Beds

Raising the bed 15-50cm/6-20in improves the drainage, makes gardening easier on your back and managing the beds a lot better.

Working from the pathway means that the beds are not trampled, and digging can be omitted. Containing manure to these areas, means using less and in wet seasons the soil is more workable.

You can raise a bed by using boards or sleepers, I use old pallet sleeves which you can often pick up for £5 and these simply stack one on top of the other if you want to go higher – these sleeves also make it a lot easier to put bird netting over the top to protect your crops!

By having raised beds, you will find that the soil heats up a lot faster, so you can start earlier with your seedlings, this also means your soil is warmer for the end of the season you can continue to grow when your neighbours have to finish, so you have just extended the growing season! Remember, if it is warmer it might need a little more water so keep an eye on them, you can do what I do and put a 3-inch mulch which keeps the water in and weeds away.

CHAPTER THREE

Practical Bits

It can be hard to fit the allotment in with work and family commitments, this is my dilemma and I need to juggle them as well as seedling and prepping and then the harvesting in amongst holidays.

So how can you juggle all of this?

Well the savvy gardener does as much as they can in the winter to ease the summer work load.

If you still find it hard put one third of your allotment into fallow by covering the soil with a thick mulch or weed suppressing membrane (don't forget that as an allotment holder two thirds need to be under cultivation. Then work on your beds section by section and if you have to save time and buy seedlings so be it! You will have done the most important part – preparing the soil! If you apply mulch you will save yourself so much time with watering as the mulch will keep the moisture in as the sun bakes the bare earth and dries it out so mulch and thickly as it has the added benefit of suppressing weeds another time-consuming job.

By preparing as much as I can in the winter when not so much is happening on the ground I save time as my large pots are washed and ready, mulch is gathered and stored, recycled, organic seed pots normally around 12 for £1 can be ordered and readied, seeds ordered, planning of the allotment is done now with what to plant where, all of this saves time in the summer when things are bursting with growth and there is watering and planting then more watering to be done. Generally, I work all day but after work I slip down to the allotment for an hour and water what needs to be watered, or pick produce or a quick weed here or there. I reserve the weekends to do any larger jobs, but even then, I spend only a couple of hours before heading out to the shops (dirt and all sometimes) to do the shopping, whip home and put the washing on etc etc it just comes down to time management, you have to work with what you can when you can.

Build your compost bin in the winter

You can use all sorts of things to build a compost bin or you can buy a new one. I have seen compost bins made of tin sheets with three sides, old pallets on three sides which allows air into the sides, pallet sleeves are great you can stack them to make them larger then when composted down remove them and place into next compost area and turn or use the compost. In the past, I have even used straw bales and stacked them two high on three sides, these break down eventually and are turned into the compost when new ones were bought. There is lots more info in the composting chapter this is just to get the mind thinking of how you can build your own compost bin.

What to put into your compost

You can put any lawn clippings in as this gives heat to your compost, spent vegetable leaves, excess vegetables that you couldn't eat, pickle or give away! You can grow comfrey to cut and put into your compost as this will speed up the breakdown process in a natural way. You can throw in cardboard that is ripped up, egg cartons, weeds (not perennial weeds or diseased materials) but anything that is raw is a good guide just put it into the compost in layers. Turn the compost every now and then to get air into it and this will encourage worms and give you a sweet-smelling compost that should be left for a year, most are ready in the summer, but you won't spread it until the autumn. There is lots more information in the composting chapter what to put in what not to put in and how and what types of composting there is.

Water

I have water butts on my shed one for each side and then one for each side of my glass house, but you can also have tanks up the end of the allotment that just catch rainwater or can be filled from the mains if you have access to mains water. The ideal number of tanks or water butts is one per four beds so that you're not lugging water too far. If you have a long allotment you can put water butts or tanks down the side and put a hose from one to the other and allow the overflow to flow down to the bottom of the garden.

Ideally you want your water to soak in not run away and using watering cans ensures that you water what needs to be watered and not the paths! A guide is 2 watering cans that hold 20 litres per square metre/yard, and a crop needs 2.5 cm or 1inch of water every 10 -14 days, so a good soak is very effective and achievable without being too laborious or wasting water. If you mulch your garden beds you will also save on water reduction. Just keep watering in mind when you are planning your garden beds!

Net covers

I use a fishing rod type of frame as it is flexible, there are lots of nets out there, but really you just need something that you can work with to cover and protect your plants from birds and pests. I found mine on eBay and was so impressed with it the next year I bought another and the year after I contacted the guy to see if I could get an even larger one! Guess what? I got a larger one! The frame reminds me of fishing rods and are joined together with joiners which makes them hoop when stuck in the ground. The net is the put over the top and held on with little clips, these clips can be unclipped to allow for easy access to weed and plant succession plants. They are brilliant, and one person is able to put it up all by themselves. Regardless of what type of netting the next problem is what do you do at the ends? Well, some people bury the ends, but after the first year I didn't want to do this because it was always a hassle when I had to open and weed, looking for another solution I came up with the idea of rolling the ends with a cane and then using tent pegs which I bought off eBay I would pin them into the ground – a perfect solution as it made it easy to lift and weed and replace.

For your soft fruits you can use a flexible net the birds won't go under for fear of being trapped and they will be able to reach the top ones but hey, we should feed the birds a little! There is plenty growing lower down and probably more than you will eat. Because these plants usually have spikes, the net naturally stays down.

CHAPTER FOUR

Companion Planting

Mixing plants together confuses insects, especially if you plant strong scented plants like the common French Marigolds with your prised vegetables. The difficulty is balancing camouflage and cultivating weeds.

The idea is to plant a quick crop that can be harvested between a widely spaced slow growing crop. For example, the widely spaced Brussel sprouts benefits from a green leafy ground cover like lettuce or early peas with a quick crop of autumn turnips.

The additional reason for companion planting is to encourage bees into your garden to pollinate your plants for without them you would have no crop to harvest so I like to keep them happy and busy!

The beneficial reasons for companion planting includes pest control, pollination, providing habitat for beneficial creatures, maximizing use of space, and to otherwise increase crop productivity.

A characteristic illustration is the combination of planted corn, squash and beans together in the same bed. The corn stalks provided support to the climber beans and light shade for the squash. The beans fixed nitrogen into the soil, making it accessible to the corn. The squash covered the ground, suppressing weeds around the other two and fended off pests.

Taller plants like corn, sunflower and okra can provide support to cucumbers and peas, planting nasturtiums near radishes improves the flavour of the root crop. Lettuce as a companion makes radishes more tender in the summer. Tarragon and dill are great for promoting the growth of cabbage family vegetables and improving their flavour. Sweet marjoram is often planted with beans, eggplants, pumpkin and cucumbers because it increases their yield.

Fragrant herbs act as insect repellents and protect their companions. For example, mint is a deterrent to ants and cabbage moth. Lavender can repel ticks. Marigold repels aphids and beetles, keeping them away from tomatoes and roses when planted together. Planting daffodils around beds of root vegetables to create a protective barrier to moles and other rodents.

Zinnias are planted with cauliflower because they attract ladybugs, which in turn control cabbage flies and other pests that would otherwise devour cauliflowers. Radishes and spinach planted in alternate rows thrive well together, the fast-growing radish with its large leaves protecting the spinach when young. Plants that attract bees and butterflies, when planted in the vegetable and fruit gardens, bring in more pollinators. This ensures better fruit set and good yield. Asters, bee balm, zinnia and yarrow are good companions in the vegetable garden.

Companion plant	Protects	Comments
Nasturtium	Cabbage, kale, cauliflower	Plant Nasturtiums as a sacrificial crop. Cabbage white butterflies will lay their eggs on Nasturtium plants, keeping caterpillars away from your Brassicas.
Mint	Cabbage, kale, cauliflower	Mint helps to deter flea beetles, which chew irregular holes in the leaves.
	Carrot	The aromatic leaves of mint help confuse carrot root fly, who find their host through scent.
	Onion	The aromatic leaves of mint help to confuse and deter onion fly.
	Radish	Mint helps to deter flea beetles, which chew irregular holes in the leaves
	Tomatoes	The smell of mint deters aphids and other pests.
Calendula (English Marigold)	Courgette	Calendula flowers are highly attractive to pollinating insects which will in turn pollinate your courgette flowers.
Summer savory	Broad beans	Summer savory helps to repel blackfly, a common pest of broad beans.
Spring onions	Carrot	Sow spring onions amongst your carrots - the smell of onion deters carrot root fly. The smell of carrots also deters onion fly from onions.
Leek	Carrot	The smell of leeks deters carrot root fly. The smell of carrots also helps deter leek moth from leeks.
Garlic	Roses	The smell of garlic helps to deter aphids.
Chives	Chrysanthemum	The onion scent will deter aphids.
	Sunflower	The onion scent will deter aphids.
	Tomatoes	The onion scent will deter aphids.
Nasturtium	French /Runner beans	Plant Nasturtiums as a sacrificial crop - aphids love them and this will lure them away from your runner beans/French beans.
	Cabbages	They're a magnet for caterpillars that will then leave the cabbages alone.

Companion plant	Protects	Comments
Mint, Chives, Thyme	Roses	The strong scent of these herbs deters aphids and blackfly.
Sweet peas	Runner beans	Sweet peas will attract pollinating insects which will in turn help to pollinate your bean flowers.
French Marigold (Tagetes patula)	Tomatoes	The pungent smell of French marigolds deters whitefly, greenfly and blackfly.
Basil	Tomatoes	Basil reportedly improves tomato flavour and the strong scent of their leaves also deters aphids. A perfect partnership in the kitchen too!
Sage	Carrots or plants in the cabbage family	Both have strong scents that drive away each other's pests.

Make sure companion plants are planted at the same time as your edible crops to prevent pests from getting a foothold.

Chervil - keeps aphids off lettuce

Chives - onion scent wards off aphids from chrysanthemums, sunflowers and tomatoes

Coriander - helps to repel aphids

Dill - attracts aphid eating beneficial insects likes hoverflies and predatory wasps

Garlic - deters aphids and is particularly good planted with roses

Tansy - strongly scented plant deters ants

Plants in the pea family - lupins, peas, beans and sweet peas benefit the soil by taking nitrogen from the air and storing it in their roots

Yarrow - this boosts vigour in other plants and accumulates phosphorous, calcium and silica, which can benefit homemade compost when plants are added to the heap. It attracts many beneficial creatures such as hoverflies and ladybirds

Not only does companion planting confuse pests, but it looks so much nicer and the bees love it which help to pollinate your produce.

Please see the companion planting chart over the next few pages for more information.

Companion planting chart

Common name	Helps	Helped by	Attracts/Repels	Comments
Alliums	Fruit trees, nightshades (tomatoes, capsicum peppers, potatoes), brassicas, carrots	Carrots, tomatoes, carrots and African spider plants (*Cleome gynandra*) together, marigolds (*Tagetes* spp.), mints	Thrips **Repels/ Distracts** -Rabbits, slugs (see Garlic), -aphids, carrot fly, - cabbage Loopers, - cabbage maggots, -Cabbage worms, - Japanese beetles	Alliums are a family of plants which include onions, garlic, leeks, shallots, chives, and others.
Asparagus	Tomatoes, parsley	Aster family flowers, dill, coriander, tomatoes, parsley, basil, comfrey, marigolds, nasturtiums	Coupled with basil seems to encourage lady bugs	
Beans, bush	Cucumber soybeans, strawberries	Celery, strawberries, grains		"Lettuce, potato, tomato, other legumes, crucifers, or cucurbits *increase* Sclerotinia" in the soil and should be avoided before and after snap beans. See the entry for "Legumes" for more info
Beans, pole		Radishes, Corn		The stalk of the corn provides a pole for the beans to grow on, which then gives nitrogen to the soil of the corn. As for the Radishes, see the entry for "Legumes" for more info

Common name	Helps	Helped by	Attracts/Repels	Comments
Beans, fava		Strawberries, Celery		See the entry for "Legumes" for more info
Beets	Broccoli, bush beans, cabbage, lettuce, kohlrabi, onions, brassicas, passion fruit	Bush beans, onions, kohlrabi, catnip, garlic, lettuce, most brassicas, mint		Good for adding minerals to the soil through composting leaves which have up to 25% magnesium. Runner or pole beans and beets stunt each other's growth.
Brassicas	Beets, onions, potatoes, cereals (e.g. Corn, wheat)	Beets, spinach, chard, Aromatic plants or plants with many blossoms, such as celery, chamomile, and marigolds. Dill, sage, peas, peppermint, spearmint, spurrey, rosemary, rye-grass, garlic, onions and potatoes. geraniums, alliums, nasturtium, borage, hyssop, tansy, tomatoes, thyme, wormwood, southernwood, beans, clover	-Repels/+distracts Wireworms	**Brassicas are a family of plants which includes broccoli, Brussels sprouts, cabbage, cauliflower, Chinese cabbage, kohlrabi, radish, and turnip.** Thyme, nasturtiums, and onion showed good resistance to cabbage worm, weevil and cabbage Looper.
Broccoli	Lettuce	Mixture of mustard, PAC Choi, and rape. Beets, dill, lettuce, mustard, onions, tomato, turnip, clover		Broccoli as a main crop intercropped with lettuce was shown to be more profitable than either crop alone. Turnip acts as a trap crop. See brassicas entry for more info
Brussels sprouts		Sage, thyme, clover, malting barley		

Common name	Helps	Helped by	Attracts/Repels	Comments
Cabbage	Beans, celery	Beans, clover, calendula/pot marigold, chamomile, larkspur, nasturtiums, dill, coriander, hyssop, onions, beets, marigolds, mint, rosemary, sage, thyme, tomatoes, lacy phacelia, Green onions with Chinese cabbage.	Snails and slugs	See brassicas entry for more info. If using clover as an intercrop, it should be sown after cabbage transplant so as not to affect crop yield. Nasturtiums repel cabbage moths
Carrots	Tomatoes, alliums, beans, leeks, lettuce, onions, passion fruit	Lettuce, alliums (chives, leeks, onions, shallots, etc.), rosemary, wormwood, sage, beans, flax	Assassin bug, lacewing, parasitic wasp, yellow jacket and other predatory wasps **-Repels/+distracts** Leek moth, onion fly	Tomatoes grow better with carrots, but may stunt the carrots' growth. Beans provide the nitrogen carrots need. Aromatic companion plants repel carrot fly. Sage, rosemary, and radishes. Alliums inter-planted with carrots confuse onion and carrot flies, use the wild carrot, Queen Anne's Lace, for the same effect. Flax produces an oil that may protect root vegetables like carrots from some pests.
Cauliflower	Beans, celery, spinach, peas	Mixture of Chinese cabbage, marigolds, rape, and sunflower. Spinach, peas		A row of spinach alternating each row of cauliflower proved mutually beneficial. See brassicas for more info. See peas about their mutualism with cauliflower.

Common name	Helps	Helped by	Attracts/Repels	Comments
Celery	Bush beans, brassicas, cucumber	Cosmos, daisies, snapdragons, leeks, tomatoes, cauliflower, cabbage, bush beans	-Repels/+distracts Whiteflies	Aster flowers can transmit the aster yellows disease
Chard	Brassicas, passion fruit			
Corn	Beans, cucurbits, soybeans, tomatoes	Sunflowers, dill, legumes (beans, peas, soybeans etc.), peanuts, cucurbits, clover, amaranth, white geranium, pigweed, lamb's quarters, morning glory, parsley, and potato, field mustard, Sudan grass		Provides beans with a trellis, is protected from predators and dryness by cucurbits, in the three sisters technique
Cucumber	Beans, kohlrabi, lettuce	Kohlrabi, nasturtiums, radishes, marigolds, sunflowers, peas, beans, chamomile, beets, carrots, dill, onions, garlic, amaranth (Amaranthus cruentus), celery, Malabar spinach	Beneficial for ground beetles -Repels/+distracts Raccoons, ants	Sow 2 or 3 radish seeds in with cucumbers to repel cucumber beetles. One study showed a 75% reduction in cucumber beetles with the concurrent seeding of amaranth. Various sprays from lettuce, asparagus, Malabar spinach, and celery were found to reduce whiteflies. See cucurbits entry for more info
Cucurbits	Corn	Corn, grain sorghum		**Cucurbits are a family of plants that includes melons, cucumbers, gourds, pumpkins, and squash**

Common name	Helps	Helped by	Attracts/Repels	Comments
Eggplant or Aubergine	Beans, peppers, tomatoes, passion fruit	Marigolds, catnip, dill, redroot pigweed, green beans, tarragon, mints, thyme		Marigolds will deter nematodes.
Kohlrabi	Onion, beets, aromatic plants, cucumbers	Beets, cucumbers		See Brassicas entry for more info
Leek	Carrots, celery, onions, tomato, passion fruit	Carrots clover,		See Alliums entry for more info
Legumes	Beets, lettuce, okra, potato, spinach, [citation needed] dill, [citation needed] cabbage, carrots, chards, eggplant, peas, tomatoes, brassicas, corn, cucumbers, grapes	Summer savory, beets, cucumbers, borage, cabbage, carrots, cauliflower, corn, larkspur, lovage, marigolds, mustards, radish, potato, peppermint, rosemary, lettuce, onion, squash, lacy Phacelia	Snails and slugs **-Repels/+distracts** Potato beetle	Hosts nitrogen-fixing bacteria, a good fertiliser for *some* plants, too much for others. Rosemary and peppermint extracts are used in organic sprays for beans. Summer savory and potatoes repel bean beetles.
Lettuce	Beets, beans, okra, onions, radish, broccoli, Carrots, passion fruit	Radish, beets, dill, kohlrabi, onions, beans, carrots, cucumbers, strawberries, broccoli thyme, nasturtiums, Alyssum, cilantro	Slugs and snails.	Mints (including hyssop, sage, and various "balms") repel slugs, a lane of lettuce and cabbages.
Mustard	Beans, broccoli, cabbage, cauliflower, fruit trees, grapes, radish, brussels' sprouts, turnips		**-Repels/+distracts** Various pests	See Brassicas entry for more info. Mustard acts as a trap crop in broccoli.

Common name	Helps	Helped by	Attracts/Repels	Comments
Nightshades		Carrots, alliums, mints (basil, oregano, etc.)		Nightshades are a family of plants which include tomatoes, tobacco, chili peppers (including bell peppers), potatoes, eggplant, and others
Okra	Sweet potato, tomatoes, peppers	Beans, lettuce, squash, sweet potato, peppers		Okra and sweet potato are mutually beneficial when planted simultaneously.
Onion	Beets, beans, brassicas, cabbage, broccoli, carrots, lettuce, cucumbers, peppers, passion fruit, strawberries. Green onions with Chinese cabbage.	Carrots, beets, brassicas, dill, lettuce, strawberries, marigolds, mints, tomatoes, summer savory, chamomile, pansy		See Alliums entry for more info
Parsnip	Fruit trees		A variety of predatory insects	Parsnip flowers left to seed will attract predatory insects to the garden and under fruit trees. The root contains Myristricin, (toxic to fruit flies, house flies, red spider mite, pea aphids), blend together 3 parsnip roots to 1 litre of water in a food processor (don't use for food after), leave overnight, strain, use within 3 days.

Common name	Helps	Helped by	Attracts/Repels	Comments
Peas	Brassicas, turnip, cauliflower, garlic,	Turnip, cauliflower, garlic, mints	**-Repels/+distracts** Potato beetle	Peas when intercropped with turnips, cauliflower, or garlic showed mutual suppression of growth, however their profit per land area used was increased.
Peppers	Okra	Beans, tomatoes, marjoram, [citation needed] okra, geraniums, petunias, sunflowers, onions crimson clover, basil, field mustard		Pepper plants like high humidity, which can be helped along by planting with dense-leaf or ground-cover plants, like marjoram and basil, but their fruit can be harmed by it... pepper plants grown together, or with tomatoes, can shelter the fruit from sunlight, and raises the humidity level. Sunflowers, when in bloom at the right time, sheltered beneficial insects which lowered thrip populations.
Potato	Brassicas, beans, corn, peas, passion fruit	Horseradish, beans, dead nettle, marigolds, peas, onion, garlic, thyme, clover	**-Repels/+distracts** Bean beetle	Horseradish increases the disease resistance of potatoes. It repels the potato bug. Garlic was shown to be more effective than fungicides on late potato blight. Peas were shown to reduce the density of Colorado potato beetles.

Common name	Helps	Helped by	Attracts/Repels	Comments
Pumpkin	Corn, beans	Buckwheat, Jimson weed, catnip, oregano, tansy, radishes, nasturtiums	Spiders, ground beetles	Radishes can be used as a trap crop against flea beetles, Nasturtiums repel squash bugs.
Radish	Squash eggplant, cucumber, lettuce, peas, beans, pole beans,	Chervil, lettuce, nasturtiums	**-Repels/+distracts** Flea beetles, cucumber beetles	Radishes can be used as a trap crop against flea beetles. Radishes grown with lettuce taste better.
Soybean		Corn, snap beans, sunflower		A mixture of corn, mungbean, and sunflower was found to rid soybeans of aphids. Snap beans act as a trap crop for Mexican bean beetles in soybeans.
Spinach	Brassicas, cauliflower, passion fruit	Strawberries, peas, beans, cauliflower		The peas and beans provide natural shade for the spinach. See cauliflower notes regarding mutualism with spinach.
Squash	Corn, beans, okra,	Beans, buckwheat, borage, catnip, tansy, radishes, marigolds, nasturtiums	Spiders, ground beetles	Radishes can be used as a trap crop against flea beetles. Marigolds and nasturtiums repel squash bugs. Marigolds repel cucumber beetles.

Common name	Helps	Helped by	Attracts/Repels	Comments
Sweet potato	Okra	Okra		Okra and sweet potato are mutually beneficial when planted at the same time.
Swedes and turnips	Peas, broccoli	Hairy vetch, peas		Turnips are a trap crop for broccoli. See peas regarding mutualism with turnips.
Tomatoes	Brassicas, broccoli, cabbage, celery, roses, peppers, asparagus	Asparagus, basil, beans, bee balm (*Monarda*), oregano, parsley, marigold, alliums, garlic, leeks, celery, geraniums, petunias, nasturtium, borage, coriander, chives, corn, dill, mustard, fenugreek, barley, carrots, eggplant, mints, okra, sage, thyme, "flower strips"	**-Repels/+distracts** Asparagus beetle	Black walnuts inhibit tomato growth, in fact they are negative allelopathic to all other nightshade plants (chili pepper, potato, tobacco, petunia) as well, because it produces juglone. Dill attracts tomato hornworm.

Growing tomatoes with Basil does not appear to enhance tomato flavour, but studies have shown that growing them around 10 inches apart can increase the yield of tomatoes by about 20%. One study shows that growing chili peppers near tomatoes in greenhouses increase tomato whitefly on the tomatoes. |

CHAPTER FIVE

Weeds

Oh, how the dreaded weeds grow so fast! Just turn your back and wham, there pops up another and another!

Most gardeners spray with pesticides, but as I am an organic gardener this is not going to happen in my allotment so with a lot of patience and determination I have found a few things very helpful and will share what I do or have tried here and then it is over to you and your hard work and determination to do battle with the weeds!

In the beginning

You have just got your allotment and you're pretty excited – well until you face the weeds! Standing there scratching your head is a good start, but the weeds are still there – that was me when, after waiting 8 years I finally got my allotment. Sadly, it was knee high with weeds, a shed that looked like the leaning tower of pizza and a cement bed which was puzzling because the cement was not allowed!

Inside of my shed I found a large piece of carpet so after cutting down an area at the back of knee to ankle height weeds I placed the carpet over the top to stop the sunlight getting to them and they will eventually die. Because you have the whole allotment to work on it is a good idea to "section it" then work on one section at a time. So, section 4 will be left for a couple of seasons while I worked on the other 3. Turning my attention to section 1 which was in front of my shed and handy access to tools I began to double dig the soil and separated soil and weeds manually, hard work I know but oh so satisfying! Once I had turned over the soil and removed the weeds I added well-rotted manure, by using well-rotted manure the weed seeds have been exhausted and helps to reduce the weeds. This is then topped up with leaf compost and left to sit while I worked on section 2!

I repeated the whole process again on section 2, what can I say it takes a lot of work in the beginning but get this part right and you will be glad you did for years in the digging future. Of course, because it is a new allotment you haven't had the opportunity to get your manure well-rotted and the first year you may have to buy it in bags just make sure it is an organic one!

Driving around, you will spot signs that state they are selling manure usually for a pound/dollar, grab some get 10 bags or so and as you fill your compost bin pour a bag into it so that you're layering a heap of weeds (there are some weeds you shouldn't put into your compost these will be listed in the compost section) then a layer of manure, this will heat up and decompose your compost faster and encourage worms the gardeners free workmen!

What is a weed?

In reality a weed is a plant where you don't want it! Yes, I have weeds in my allotment it can't be helped seeds blow in from all around, but I also have poppies and foxgloves growing everywhere and the first year I had my allotment I kept them because the bees loved them but then next year I had so many that there wasn't a lot of room for my veg!

Heartbreakingly I had to start pulling them up and it really did make me sad at first, but now if they are in my veg bed, I transplant them to the boarders (after all I still want the bees to visit and they are so pretty!)

We have creeping buttercup, and this produces roots everywhere and is really hard to get rid of, years down the track and we are still pulling this up! If you have bare soil a weed will grow! Hang on, that is so important let me repeat it...

If you have bare soil a weed will grow

So what is the answer? Well, time for section 3 in my allotment what did I do? I covered it with really, really thick leaf mulch! Most allotments are given this leaf mulch from the councils freely our allotment group gets 2 truckloads a year, now not everyone uses it but we sure as heck do! I do one barrow load dump go back get another and same thing dump – I don't spread it, my mulch is a barrow load thick, so yes, it takes a lot, but it blocks out the sun and if any weeds grow through they are so weak they are easy to pull out when they do. Most importantly, don't let your weeds produce flowers if you do then you can count a good 7 years of weed pulling to add to your list of chores!

I remember my very experienced allotment neighbour who in the beginning was very kind, but when we put down the leaf mulch she went nuts at me saying that won't stop the weeds and you don't know what is in that mulch. Well the following year where I had put the leaf mulch I had about a dozen weeds compared to other allotments who hadn't used it and my allotment was full of worms! These marvellous creatures work their way up and down in and out all through the soil eating the rotting mulch pulling it through the soil and pooping it out to naturally feed my soil, what wonderful and treasured creatures they are!

So, to recap

After weeding, I sectioned my allotment – section 4 left for next summer, section 3 heavily mulched and left for winter digging over and worked and concentrated on section 1 and 2 with double digging.

By the time I had finished section 2, section 1 was ready for planting, then section 2 followed shortly after. Just do a bit at a time and suddenly you have done it all without realising it and doesn't it feel good!

CHAPTER SIX

Composting

Composting is the best, easiest way to recycle freely and it will replenish your garden! Pretty much anything goes – anything that has lived once or was made from a living thing can be composted provided it has all-natural components it will break down. Compost is key to gardening, you need it to feed the soil, you need it to encourage worms, you need it to help keep moisture in the soil for your plants to remain healthy. It is easy to compost, start with vegetable scraps, dead leaves, grass clippings, shredded cardboard etc.

But…

Be warned, there are some things you must not compost because if you do, you will spread it all over your allotment!

Poop
You can add horse, cow, chicken or rabbit droppings to your compost pile. Once broken down, they add nutrients and organic matter that will feed and improve your soil. Warning don't add poop from your cats and/or dogs, this waste may contain microorganisms and parasites that you don't want transferred to what you will be eating.

Tea and Coffee Bags

You can add coffee grounds and tea leaves absolutely belong in your compost pile. They deliver large quantities of nitrogen, phosphorous and potassium, these are all elements that are vital for your plants. You can't add the bags, you must remove them from the bags.

Onion and Citrus Peelings

You can't add onion and citrus peelings to your compost because the natural chemicals and acidity in them can kill your worms and other microorganisms, this will then slow down the breakdown process in your compost pile.

Meat and fish

Yes, meat and fish are organic and yes, they will break down and they would add nutrients to the soil, but you can't add them to your compost heap because the odour will draw rats, mice, cats and other wild animals to your compost heap and eat it and besides if the local roaming animals didn't eat it all imagine the smell (it wouldn't make you popular with your allotment neighbours!).

Paper

Organic papers like soy-ink newspapers, paper towels, tissues and shredded cardboard can go in your compost heap. But glossy magazines, bright and colourful printed papers and plastic like papers can't go in your compost heap as they have been treated with a variety of toxins to make them look pretty and you don't want toxins in your compost heap. Another form of paper are those sticky labels they put on apples and other fruit and vegetables! Remove them as they are not biodegradable!

Ashes

Coal fires or charcoal-briquet fires can't be added to your compost heap because of the amount of sulfur it contains this would make your soil extremely acidic besides many charcoal briquettes are chemically treated and you don't want that leaching into your vegetables. You can add ash from a wood fire, but only in small proportions, you don't want to overload your soil.

Sawdust

If it is untreated natural wood, then yes, you can add this to your compost heap, but if the wood is treated in any way; varnish, stain, paint, pressure treatment, then you can't add this to your compost heap because the toxic components such as arsenic and cadmium won't break down and can leach into your soil and affect microorganisms and your plants and you certainly don't want to be eating those toxins!

Size of waste

The smaller the waste product the faster it will break down, so large branches and thick stalks will take an extremely long-time compost, so you need to chop or chip them smaller or set aside a long-term compost heap in an out of the spot and leave it for years

The true way to compost

An effective compost heap is a balance of dry or brown carbon items (such as leaves, straw, or paper) and wet or green things that contain nitrogen (such as grass cuttings, food scraps or rabbit droppings).

So, if you have mowed the lawn, put it in then follow it up with shredded cardboard, manure (remember I said to buy 10 or so bags? Here is why) then kitchen vegetable peelings etc. add a little water to the mix (so keep the water from the teapot it can all go in provided there are no bags!) if you have straw that can go in as well, keeping it in layers will help to keep a balance and decompose faster.

Keep it small

Like I said earlier, the smaller the waste product begins at the faster it will decompose so chop before you add to your compost heap, shed if you can, then you can be using it in a short time rather than leaving it for many months to break down

Air and Water

Adding air to your heap helps to distribute the heat and keeping it watered (not soggy) will keep the heat locked in. Use your garden fork to turn the heap or if you have a tumbler give it a turn each time you go down to it.

It is the balance of air and moisture in the compost heap encourages the microorganisms to do their job in breaking down your compost air and water along with the waste is all they need to thrive.

Hot and cold composting

Hot composting is where you turn the pile on a regular basis say once a week as this encourages it to heat up and you need the heat to kill weed seeds and other pathogens. Cold composting is what most gardeners do, layer the heap and allow it to decompose on its own, this of course takes a lot longer to break down and the weed seeds are left without any light to grow so they die (only the weed seeds at the top of the pile will grow).

Composting weeds

Important rule: _don't compost weeds that have gone to seed!_

If you are going to throw weeds into your compost heap, be sure that they haven't set seed.

Dandelions are one of the worst! These seeds sit in your compost until you spread your compost all over your garden beds, and, boom! You've got a weed infestation. If your weeds have gone to seed, throw them in the trash or bag them.

Weeds and plants that Spread by Runners

Mint, raspberry canes, bindweed, dock, and switchgrass. If, when you're pulling it from your allotment, you end up pulling a long root that attaches itself to other plants -- don't compost it, otherwise you'll be pulling it out of your allotment forever.

Composting the pesky weeds

Weeds that spread by runners need to be killed with lots of heat otherwise they will bounce back to life, even if it is a tiny little bit – it wants to survive even if you don't want it to! So you need to outsmart them in an environmentally friendly way by using "solar power" which is used for controlling pests such as soilborne plant pathogens including fungi, bacteria, nematodes, and insect and mite pests along with weed seed and seedlings. How? Put them into a black bag with no holes double bag if you like then put it in a sunny out of the way spot and leave it for about 4 months, then open it and if you can't distinguish anything then you can add it to your compost heap and it won't cause you problems year after year.

Manure compost and soil additives

Celery, potatoes and runner beans love soils which have plenty of freshly dug in well-rotted animal manure and garden compost. Soils enriched in this way are not good for root crops in particular carrot chicory and parsnip because the roots will fork in search of the manure, so it is better to let crops like runner beans take advantage of the freshly manured land then follow next season with carrots etc as they will grow faster and larger in richer and more moisture retaining soils that have very well-rotted down organic matter.

The application of lime should be the season before brassicas as this gives the longest time before planting potatoes whose skins will become marked with the disease scab in alkaline (chalky and lime bearing) soils.

Types of compost bins

We like to have our compost looking tidy or neat, particularly when it is visible. Fortunately, there are a variety of different types of compost bins for all sorts of situations like pallet bins, tumblers which make turning the compost easier, towers for small spaces, and my favourite worm composters that will make fast, odourless work of uncooked table scraps.

Wire Compost Bin: Faultless for composting anything because it encourages air flow, throw in leaves, grass clippings, garden trimmings and kitchen scraps. It takes around 10 minutes to make, requires barely any tools, simply grab 3 stakes and some chicken wire. Make a 3-sided square in the position you have allocated for it and wrap some chicken wire around the stakes or thread the stakes through the netting and you have an open compost giving you access to the heap for turning.

Plastic Storage Bin Composter: Perfect for the small gardener or apartment situations the plastic composter will work because of the heat it will generate but don't over water because it has nowhere to run!

Trash Can: Many years ago, I got a steel can and punched holes in it, I chose it because it was small, and I had a tiny garden back then I layered the compost and to turn the compost I just rolled the can around a few times and stood it back up!

Sheet Composting: This is where you build layers of compost where you intend to plant! The upside of this is that you don't have to turn it, the downside is that it does look untidy at first.

Vermicomposting: I love my worms and a worm farm is so easy to care for! Placed in a dry out of the sun position you can feed your daily kitchen scraps to them (I always left the water in but don't overdo it with the water). You will be surprised at how fast they can munch their way through everything you feed to them! They sit on the first floor (bottom floor is where the liquid drains to) a small amount of compost (that fills the tray) and the worms live in the first floor, the next tray sits on top and that is where you put your scraps. They munch their way through pooping and multiplying as they do and the liquid in the bottom can be drained away and used as liquid fertiliser for pot plants or as a boost for your plants. Eventually they eat their way up and the second tray fills, you can then empty the first tray and use as manure on your plants and place the now empty tray to the top again and repeat the process. Just remember onions, citrus and garlic are not to go in because they will kill your worms!

CHAPTER SEVEN

Crop Rotation

Crop rotation helps to avoid diseases such as club root which will multiply rapidly if you grow the same crops in the same soil, but it doesn't end there if you grow the same crops in the same beds they will deplete the soil of nutrients as each group of vegetables require different sets of nutrients from the soil.

Vegetable Families

Alliums: Onion, garlic, shallot, leek

Brassicas: Brussels sprouts, cabbage, cauliflower, kale, kohl-rabi, oriental greens, radish, swede and turnips

Cucurbitaceae: courgettes, marrows

Legumes: Peas, broad beans, French and runner beans

Potato (Solanum): Potato, tomato

Roots: Beetroot, carrot, celeriac, celery, Florence fennel, parsley, parsnip (swedes and turnips are brassicas)

For example: first year, a bed that has grown other crops would then in its second year grow brassicas then the third year should grow root crops.

If you have a large enough garden the whole rotation scheme can be expanded by separating peas and beans (the legumes) from the other crops, this gives a four-year crop rotation and professionals work their cropping schemes to the lever of perfection, but for the home gardener a three-year crop rotation is sufficient as a two-year minimum is required to not deplete the soil and avoid diseases.

You can devise your own rotation, just remember to keep a record of what you have grown, (we have supplied a section where you can do this later in the book) where and when. I have created below a typical crop rotation process, which also includes when to add compost or grow green manures.

Firstly, divide your growing area into four or more sections. Then divide your crops into families (see above). If you keep the plants in these families together (such as potatoes and tomatoes), but move them around the different sections, each year, you will have a successful crop rotation.

A simple chart which shows an example of a 4-year rotation. It includes summer, spring planting, then autumn, winter planting, and when to apply compost and grow green manures.

Don't forget to leave bed space for perennials – such as rhubarb, asparagus and herbs, such as thyme, marjoram and mint (although the latter is best grown in a container to prevent it spreading!)

After the examples you will have the opportunity to record your crop rotations.

Year one

Plot 1	Plot 2	Plot 3	Plot 4
Spring and summer planting:			
Potatoes Tomatoes, courgettes	Carrots, Parsnips, Beetroot, Celery, Spinach, Chard	brassicas, Such as cabbage, Broccoli, Cauliflower	Peas, Beans
Autumn planting:			
Onions, Leeks, Garlic (or green manure)	Green manure to break up soil	Winter brassicas, such as kale, Sprouts Add compost to this plot in spring and summer	

Example 1 first year planting

Year two

Plot 1	Plot 2	Plot 3	Plot 4
Spring and summer planting:			
Peas, Beans	Potatoes Tomatoes, courgettes	Carrots, Parsnips, Beetroot, Celery, Spinach, Chard	brassicas, such as cabbage, Broccoli, Cauliflower
Autumn planting:			
	Onions, Leeks, Garlic (or green manure)	Green manure to break up soil	Winter brassicas, such as kale, Sprouts Add compost to this plot in spring and summer

Example 2 second year planting

Year three

Plot 1	Plot 2	Plot 3	Plot 4
Spring and summer planting:			
brassicas, such as cabbage, Broccoli, Cauliflower	Peas, Beans	Potatoes Tomatoes, courgettes	Carrots, Parsnips, Beetroot, Celery, Spinach, Chard
Autumn planting:			
Winter brassicas, such as kale, Sprouts Add compost to this plot in spring and summer		Onions, Leeks, Garlic (or green manure)	Green manure to break up soil

Example 3 third year planting

Year four

Plot 1	Plot 2	Plot 3	Plot 4
Spring and summer planting:			
Carrots, Parsnips, Beetroot, Celery, Spinach, Chard	brassicas, such as cabbage, Broccoli, Cauliflower	Peas, Beans	Potatoes Tomatoes, courgettes
Autumn planting:			
Green manure to break up soil	Winter brassicas, such as kale, Sprouts Add compost to this plot in spring and summer		Onions, Leeks, Garlic (or green manure)

Example 4 fourth year planting

Year one

Plot 1	Plot 2	Plot 3	Plot 4
Spring and summer planting:			
Autumn planting:			

Year two

Plot 1	Plot 2	Plot 3	Plot 4
Spring and summer planting:			
Autumn planting:			

Year three

Plot 1	Plot 2	Plot 3	Plot 4
Spring and summer planting:			
Autumn planting:			

Year four

Plot 1	Plot 2	Plot 3	Plot 4
Spring and summer planting:			
Autumn planting:			

CHAPTER EIGHT

Start Planning

You can never plan everything, and things always turn out a little different to what you thought it would, but it is always a good idea to work out what you want and where you are going to put it!

Think about what has to be covered, what doesn't, what grows tallest so that it doesn't shade out other plants that need full sun. Then you have things like where are your paths going to go that allow easy travelling for you, how will you get water to your plants. There are lots of things to think about, but one thing you will learn very quickly…

You will change your mind often until you're happy!

Oh, and don't expect to do it all in the one year or season either! It takes time, the first season you will work out what worked and didn't work for you and you will if you use this book correctly, make notes of what you want to change for next season. The allotment is a work in progress that goes on forever! It always has a to do list! You are now chained to your allotment for as long as you want to be. You can be happy in knowing that gardening is the best form of exercise you can do, so now you can get your exercises done in a productive and satisfying way. Many of my allotment neighbours are there all day with their packed lunches and thermos packed daily in their sheds and seat in the shade with gum boots by the door ready for the day ahead.

You want to draw on the pages purposely left blank here for you the shape of your allotment, then add in where your shed, glass house, compost heap and water butts will go. From here you will realise just where you will need the paths to go so that you can access all of these easily. Now you want to mark north and south as this will help you to work out which way your rows should face for maximum sun and growth, add any trees on your allotment and any other permanent features you have. With the space that is left you can now decide where your beds are to go – this is the ground work of your planning

Here is the list to help draw your allotment don't worry if takes several goes, I have included enough pages to help decide how you want it all – I changed mine several times over!

- Boundary
- Shed
- Glass house
- Compost heap
- Water butts
- Trees
- Mark North and South
- Any other permanent features
- Paths
- Garden beds

The next few pages are for you to draw and plan…

SUE MESSRUTHER

CHAPTER NINE

Plant details

Deciding what to grow is a personal choice, then remembering which ones did better or ones you vow to never grow again, even things to do differently next time can all be recorded to help produce for future years. I found keeping a record of what I planted so handy! It meant that I could plant better/heavier producing or improved disease/pest resistant vegetables in my area.

Vegetable Name:

Variety Planted:

Date seeds sown:

Germination period:

Seedlings planted out:

Harvest:

Comments:

Vegetable Name:

Variety Planted:

Date seeds sown:

Germination period:

Seedlings planted out:

Harvest:

Comments:

Vegetable Name:

Variety Planted:

Date seeds sown:

Germination period:

Seedlings planted out:

Harvest:

Comments:

Vegetable Name:

_____

Variety Planted:

_____

Date seeds sown:

_____

Germination period:

_____

Seedlings planted out:

_____

Harvest:

_____

Comments:

_____

Vegetable Name:

_____

Variety Planted:

_____

Date seeds sown:

_____

Germination period:

_____

Seedlings planted out:

_____

Harvest:

_____

Comments:

_____

Vegetable Name:

Variety Planted:

Date seeds sown:

Germination period:

Seedlings planted out:

Harvest:

Comments:

Vegetable Name:

Variety Planted:

Date seeds sown:

Germination period:

Seedlings planted out:

Harvest:

Comments:

Vegetable Name:

Variety Planted:

Date seeds sown:

Germination period:

Seedlings planted out:

Harvest:

Comments:

Vegetable Name:

Variety Planted:

Date seeds sown:

Germination period:

Seedlings planted out:

Harvest:

Comments:

Vegetable Name:

Variety Planted:

Date seeds sown:

Germination period:

Seedlings planted out:

Harvest:

Comments:

Vegetable Name:

Variety Planted:

Date seeds sown:

Germination period:

Seedlings planted out:

Harvest:

Comments:

ORGANIC ALLOTMENT JOURNAL PLANNER

Vegetable Name:

Variety Planted:

Date seeds sown:

Germination period:

Seedlings planted out:

Harvest:

Comments:

Vegetable Name:

Variety Planted:

Date seeds sown:

Germination period:

Seedlings planted out:

Harvest:

Comments:

Vegetable Name:

Variety Planted:

Date seeds sown:

Germination period:

Seedlings planted out:

Harvest:

Comments:

Vegetable Name:

Variety Planted:

Date seeds sown:

Germination period:

Seedlings planted out:

Harvest:

Comments:

Vegetable Name:

_____

Variety Planted:

_____

Date seeds sown:

_____

Germination period:

_____

Seedlings planted out:

_____

Harvest:

_____

Comments:

_____

Vegetable Name:

_____

Variety Planted:

_____

Date seeds sown:

_____

Germination period:

_____

Seedlings planted out:

_____

Harvest:

_____

Comments:

_____

Vegetable Name:

Variety Planted:

Date seeds sown:

Germination period:

Seedlings planted out:

Harvest:

Comments:

Vegetable Name:

Variety Planted:

Date seeds sown:

Germination period:

Seedlings planted out:

Harvest:

Comments:

Vegetable Name:

_____

Variety Planted:

_____

Date seeds sown:

_____

Germination period:

_____

Seedlings planted out:

_____

Harvest:

_____

Comments:

_____

Vegetable Name:

_____

Variety Planted:

_____

Date seeds sown:

_____

Germination period:

_____

Seedlings planted out:

_____

Harvest:

_____

Comments:

_____

Vegetable Name:

_____

Variety Planted:

_____

Date seeds sown:

_____

Germination period:

_____

Seedlings planted out:

_____

Harvest:

_____

Comments:

_____

Vegetable Name:

_____

Variety Planted:

_____

Date seeds sown:

_____

Germination period:

_____

Seedlings planted out:

_____

Harvest:

_____

Comments:

_____

Vegetable Name:

Variety Planted:

Date seeds sown:

Germination period:

Seedlings planted out:

Harvest:

Comments:

Vegetable Name:

Variety Planted:

Date seeds sown:

Germination period:

Seedlings planted out:

Harvest:

Comments:

Vegetable Name:
_____

Variety Planted:
_____

Date seeds sown:
_____

Germination period:
_____

Seedlings planted out:
_____

Harvest:
_____

Comments:
_____

Vegetable Name:
_____

Variety Planted:
_____

Date seeds sown:
_____

Germination period:
_____

Seedlings planted out:
_____

Harvest:
_____

Comments:
_____

ORGANIC ALLOTMENT JOURNAL PLANNER

Vegetable Name:
_____

Variety Planted:
_____

Date seeds sown:
_____

Germination period:
_____

Seedlings planted out:
_____

Harvest:
_____

Comments:
_____

Vegetable Name:
_____

Variety Planted:
_____

Date seeds sown:
_____

Germination period:
_____

Seedlings planted out:
_____

Harvest:
_____

Comments:
_____

Vegetable Name:

Variety Planted:

Date seeds sown:

Germination period:

Seedlings planted out:

Harvest:

Comments:

Vegetable Name:

Variety Planted:

Date seeds sown:

Germination period:

Seedlings planted out:

Harvest:

Comments:

Vegetable Name:

_____

Variety Planted:

_____

Date seeds sown:

_____

Germination period:

_____

Seedlings planted out:

_____

Harvest:

_____

Comments:

_____

Vegetable Name:

_____

Variety Planted:

_____

Date seeds sown:

_____

Germination period:

_____

Seedlings planted out:

_____

Harvest:

_____

Comments:

_____

Vegetable Name:
_____

Variety Planted:
_____

Date seeds sown:
_____

Germination period:
_____

Seedlings planted out:
_____

Harvest:
_____

Comments:

_____

Vegetable Name:
_____

Variety Planted:
_____

Date seeds sown:
_____

Germination period:
_____

Seedlings planted out:
_____

Harvest:
_____

Comments:

_____

Vegetable Name:

___

Variety Planted:

___

Date seeds sown:

___

Germination period:

___

Seedlings planted out:

___

Harvest:

___

Comments:

___

Vegetable Name:

___

Variety Planted:

___

Date seeds sown:

___

Germination period:

___

Seedlings planted out:

___

Harvest:

___

Comments:

___

Vegetable Name:

Variety Planted:

Date seeds sown:

Germination period:

Seedlings planted out:

Harvest:

Comments:

Vegetable Name:

Variety Planted:

Date seeds sown:

Germination period:

Seedlings planted out:

Harvest:

Comments:

Vegetable Name:

Variety Planted:

Date seeds sown:

Germination period:

Seedlings planted out:

Harvest:

Comments:

Vegetable Name:

Variety Planted:

Date seeds sown:

Germination period:

Seedlings planted out:

Harvest:

Comments:

Vegetable Name:

Variety Planted:

Date seeds sown:

Germination period:

Seedlings planted out:

Harvest:

Comments:

Vegetable Name:

Variety Planted:

Date seeds sown:

Germination period:

Seedlings planted out:

Harvest:

Comments:

CHAPTER TEN

Beds

Remember, youu need to rotate garden beds? Well trying to remember what you grew and where in which bed becomes blurred after all it was a year ago! It was for this very reason I needed this journal myself because those scrap bits of paper are lost forever!

Now you can record what you planted and where simply…

- Draw your bed
- Name it
- Then you can fill in what you planted.

This will help you to rotate, *for crop rotation, please refer to that section*.

Bed Name: _____

Date:

_____

Bed Name: _____

Date:

_____

SUE MESSRUTHER

Bed Name: _____

Date:

_____

ORGANIC ALLOTMENT JOURNAL PLANNER

Bed Name: _____

Date:

_____

Bed Name: _____

Date:

_____

Bed Name: _____

Date:

_____

SUE MESSRUTHER

Bed Name: _____

Date:

_____

Bed Name: _____

Date:

_____

Bed Name: _____

Date:

_____

Bed Name: _____

Date:

_____

Bed Name: _____

Date:

_____

Bed Name: _____

Date:

_____

Monthly Jobs

Every month there is always something to do in the allotment and with careful planning you can help divide some of the work load in the months that are very busy.

Each of the months has a:

- Seed sowing guide

- Plants to plant outside

- What can be harvested

- Other notes which are jobs to be done

Make sure you take time to enjoy your allotment I have a camp stove in my shed for the kettle to make hot cups of tea and a camp toilet (you can't have one without the other!). I find there is nothing more pleasurable than to sit on the bench and look at the hard work I have done while drinking a coffee or munching on something from the garden.

January

Time to sow the following seeds:

Rocket   Winter lettuce

You can plant out now:

Rhubarb   Blackberries   Gooseberries

Raspberries

You can harvest this month:

Harvesting is small because of temperatures and daylight.

Brussel sprouts   Kale   Winter Lettuce

Other notes:

Clear any dead plants from your plots

Clean flower pots, seed trays and tools ready for next year

Draw up soil around your brussels sprouts or stake them for support

Order seeds for next year

Start planning your plots for next year with crop rotation

Tidy shed/ storage, check they are secure and weather proof.

February

Time to sow the following seeds:

Autumn cabbage	Peppers	Radish
Kale	Tomatoes	Lettuce
Leeks	Aubergines	Rocket
Spring onions	Broad beans	Spinach
Cucumber	Peas	

You can plant out now:

Garlic	Shallots	Rhubarb
Onion sets	Broad beans	Jerusalem artichokes

You can harvest this month:

Understandably, there is nothing to harvest spend time preparing so you can reap the rewards at harvest later in the year.

Other notes:

Slugs and snails are still lurking, but they will be under boards, pots and other such items that provide shelter, you can collect them and remove them, if you are going to kill them a quick death is human even to these foragers who can eat a crop in 20 seconds.

Net brassicas, onion sets and your seed beds if outside against the hungry birds that are around looking for their next meal!

Digging should be completed by the end of January as the first preparation step for planting out.

Divide and cover rhubarb crowns

Feed asparagus plants and prepare new beds.

Prune autumn raspberries, general tidy up around the plants and I put leaf mould around them as well from my compost reserves.

Chit your early potatoes on a cool ledge where they can receive sunlight without getting hot

March

Time to sow the following seeds:

Seeds for Indoors:

Aubergines	Coriander	Peppers
Celeriac	Cucumber	Sweet corn
Chives	Globe artichokes	Tomatoes

Seeds for Outdoors:

Basil	Chard	Marjoram
Beetroot	Chicory	Mint
Borage	Courgettes	Onion sets
Broad beans	Dill	Parsnip
Broccoli	Fennel	Peas
Brussel sprouts	French beans	Rocket
Cabbages	Kale	Spinach
Calabrese	Kohl Rabi	Spring onions
Carrots	Leeks	Swiss chard
Celery	Lettuce	Turnips

You can plant out now:

Asparagus crowns	Currants	Onion sets
Bay	Early potatoes	Peas
Blackberries	Garlic	Raspberries
Broad beans	Green manures	Shallots
Cauliflower	Jerusalem artichokes	Strawberries

You can harvest this month:

Harvesting begins this month, even if they are small you can begin and then plant again for a continuous crop.

Broccoli	Kale	Rhubarb
Cabbage	Leeks	Rosemary
Calabrese	Lettuce	Spinach
Cauliflower	Parsnips	

Other notes:

Chit all forms of potatoes on a cool ledge where they can get sunlight without heating up too much

Plastic bottles with the bottom cut off make great individual glass houses and I use these often, particularly if I am late planting out or if I want to bring a few forward a little faster for cropping first.

Net your young plants to protect from the birds they will pull up seedlings looking for a seed!

Feed your winter crops

Net all of your fruit bushes or you won't get anything before the birds feast on them!

Prepare climbing frames

Prune autumn raspberries if you haven't already done so, include mature blueberries, currants and gooseberries as well.

Rake seed beds before sowing outdoor seeds and sprinkle with fertilizer now before the seeds go in.

You can now remove the cloches from rhubarb

Tidy plot edges

Of course, there is always weeding to do!

April

Time to sow the following seeds:

Seeds for Indoors:

Aubergines	Fennel	Runner beans
Celeriac	French beans	Squash
Chives	Globe artichokes	Sweet corn
Coriander	Kale	Tomatoes
Courgettes	Peppers	
Cucumber	Pumpkin	

Seeds for Outdoors:

Basil	Cauliflower	Kohl Rabi
Beetroot	Celery	Leeks
Borage	Chard	Lettuce
Broad beans	Chicory	Marjoram
Broccoli	Courgettes	Mint
Brussel sprouts	Dill	Onion sets
Cabbages	Fennel	Parsnip
Calabrese	French beans	Peas
Carrots	Kale	Radish

Rocket

Spring onion

Swiss chard

Spinach

Spring onions

Turnips

Sprouting broccoli

You can plant out now:

Asparagus crowns

Globe artichoke

Peas

Bay

Green manures

Potatoes

Blackberries

Jerusalem artichokes

Radish

Broad beans

Kale

Raspberries

Cauliflower

Kohl Rabi

Shallots

Currants

Lettuce

Sprouting broccoli

Early potatoes

Onion sets

Strawberries

Garlic

Oriental leaves

You can harvest this month:

Harvesting is a wonderful time, all the fresh food to fill your plates, but remember to keep sowing for a continuous crop.

Broccoli

Kale

Rhubarb

Cabbage

Leeks

Rosemary

Calabrese

Lettuce

Spinach

Cauliflower

Parsnips

Other notes:

Earth up your potatoes

This is the last opportunity to feed currant bushes, blueberries and strawberries, so if you haven't done so do it now (unless you fed them in March).

Protect small plants and seedlings with netting. I use a great hooped system that is easy to unclick and pull back the netting to weed or harvest.

Remove rhubarb cloches if you haven't yet.

Stake and support peas and beans

Start herb beds

As always, keep weeding

May

Time to sow the following seeds:

Basil	Globe artichokes	Rocket
Beetroot	Kale	Runner beans
Cabbage	Kohl Rabi	Squash
Calabrese	Lettuce	Sugar snap peas
Cauliflower	Oriental leaves	Swedes
Coriander	Parsley	Sweet corn
Courgettes	Peppers	Tomatoes
Cucumber	Potatoes	Turnip
Fennel	Pumpkins	
French beans	Purple sprouting broccoli	

You can harvest this month:

Enjoy the fruits of your labour, you can pick when young you don't have to wait, but remember to keep sowing for a continuous crop.

Broccoli	Garlic	Parsnips
Cabbage	Kale	Peas
Calabrese	Leeks	Soft fruits as they ripen
Cauliflower	Lettuce	Spinach

Other notes:

Check for pests and diseases on your beans so you can nip it in the butt early

Earth up potatoes again, you need to keep the daylight away from the growing potatoes you can also put mulch all around them for added protection (in the past I have grown them in straw which is a no dig method – when the leaves turned yellow and ready for harvest I just lifted the straw!).

Hoe your weeds and keep on top of them because in this heat they soon grow faster than your plants!

Mulch fruit crops and trees

Net your soft fruits and fruit trees now if you haven't done so or the birds will peck at them while still green.

Pinch out broad bean and pea tips once pods begin to form so that the energy goes into fruiting.

Pull out raspberry suckers/runners and now is the time to put straw under them.

Remove side shoots from tomatoes

Stop pulling rhubarb at the end of may

Thin carrots, beetroot and fennel

Water and then mulch all beds to help keep the moisture where it is needed and keep the roots cool.

June

Time to sow the following seeds:

Beetroot	Globe artichokes	Rocket
Broccoli	Kale	Runner beans
Cabbage	Kohl Rabi	Sage
Calabrese	Lettuce	Squash
Carrots	Oriental leaves	Sugar snap peas
Cauliflower	Parsley	Swedes
Chilies	Peas	Sweet corn
Coriander	Peppers	Swiss chard
Courgettes	Potatoes	Thyme
Cucumber	Pumpkins	Tomatoes
Fennel	Purple sprouting broccoli	Turnip
French beans	Radish	

You can plant out now:

Asparagus crowns	Broad beans	Cauliflower
Aubergines	Broccoli	Celeriac
Bay	Brussels sprouts	Celery
Blackberries	Cabbages	Chilies

Courgettes	Kale	Squash
Cucumbers	Leeks	Strawberries
Currants	Peas	Sweet corn
Endives	Pumpkins	Sweet peppers
French & runner beans	Raspberries	Tomatoes
Jerusalem artichokes	Shallots	

You can harvest this month:

As the sun stays out longer now we have more time for planting and harvesting, even if the produce is small you can pick and then plant again for a continuous crop.

Asparagus	Early potatoes	Radishes
Bay	Fennel	Rhubarb
Beetroot	Garlic	Rosemary
Broad beans	Kale	Sage
Broccoli	Leeks	Soft fruits as they ripen
Calabrese	Lettuce	Spinach
Carrots	Marjoram	Strawberries
Cauliflower	Mint	Summer Cabbage
Coriander	Parsnips	
Dill	Peas	

Other notes:

Earth up potatoes to keep the daylight away from the growing potatoes

Feed blueberries

Net your brassicas and all fruits to protect from pests.

Pinch out broad bean and pea tips once pods begin to form.

Remove side shoots from tomatoes

Prune mildew out of gooseberries and allow air to circulate through the bush to avoid this from happening again.

Remove raspberry suckers.

Stake French and runner beans with strong supports and netting.

Stake and cross string broad beans for support

Stop cutting asparagus by end of June, now feed them.

Tie up sweet peas to support trellis

Thin carrots

Trim and tidy paths

Water and then mulch all beds to help keep the moisture where it is needed and keep the roots cool.

Hoe any weeds in garden beds

July

Time to sow the following seeds:

Beetroot	Fennel	Radish
Broccoli	French beans	Rocket
Cabbage	Kale	Runner beans
Calabrese	Kohl Rabi	Swedes
Carrots	Lettuce	Swiss chard
Cauliflower	Oriental leaves	Turnips
Chicory	Peas	
Endive	Purple sprouting broccoli	

You can plant out now:

Broccoli	Endives	Peas
Brussels sprouts	French & runner beans	Beetroot
Cabbages	Kale	Sprouting broccoli
Cauliflower	Leeks	

You can harvest this month:

Harvesting is plentiful this month one of the richest months be careful to plant a continuous crop, but don't over glut you don't want to waste food.

Bay	Early potatoes	Peppers
Beetroot	Fennel	Radishes
Blackberries	Garlic	Raspberries
Broad beans	Gooseberries	Red and black currents
Broccoli	Kale	Rhubarb
Calabrese	Leeks	Rosemary
Carrots	Lettuce	Sage
Cauliflower	Marjoram	Spinach
Coriander	Mint	Strawberries
Cucumbers	Parsnips	Summer Cabbage
Dill	Peas	Tomatoes

Other notes:

Check brassicas for butterfly eggs.

Check asparagus for beetles.

Cut back the old leaves on strawberry plants, feed them and remove runners and pot them up to make new plants.

Cut out fruited and weak canes in your raspberries

Draw up soil around stems of brassicas and sweetcorn to keep them stable as they start to get top heavy.

Dry herbs or pick and chop, then freeze them (you can put them into ice cube trays with a little water, then when frozen empty them into a freezer bag and freeze a new batch).

Keep earthing up potatoes and mulch the furrows.

Feed tomatoes and peppers every 10 to 14 days.

Keep hoeing those weeds, they are easy to get up when they are small!

You can begin to lift onions, shallots and garlic, then dry them in the sun or on a bench in the glass house just space them out so air can get to them.

Pick vegetables while they are young and tender, particularly courgettes as they can grow massively over night!

Pinch out tomato side shoots

Protect cauliflower heads from the sun by covering them with the outside leaves, peg these together or tie them

Spray liquid seaweed on peas and beans to feed them.

_Do_ a summer prune on your gooseberries and currants to keep them in check and allow air to circulate around the centre of the bushes.

Watch out for mildew on all plants.

Water and mulch as necessary – it is far better to deep water plants and cover with mulch than to sprinkle a little water each day on them (this encourages surface roots).

August

Time to sow the following seeds:

Broccoli	Kohl Rabi	Rocket
Cabbage	Lettuce	Spinach
Carrots	Oriental leaves	Swiss chard
Kale	Radish	

You can plant out now:

Broccoli	Kale
Cauliflower	Strawberries

You can harvest this month:

Pick often for things like peas and younger for sweet tasting veg like beetroot.

Beetroot	Kale	Soft fruits
Broad beans	Leeks	Red and black currents
Broccoli	Lettuce	Rhubarb
Carrots	Parsnips	Spinach
Cauliflower	Peas	Strawberries
Cucumbers	Peppers	Summer Cabbage
Potatoes	Radishes	Tomatoes

Other notes:

Make sure your beans and peas are well supported.

Continue to pinch out tomato side shoots

Cut back lavender – you can tie bunches together and put on the windowsill to deter flies or make lavender bags for your draws.

Deadhead flowers as it lengthens the growing season.

Dry garlic and onions in the sun before storing

Earth up celery and potatoes.

Feed peppers and tomatoes every 10-14 days.

Hoe the weeds

Mulch after watering

Plant out strawberry runners

Sow green manure crops in empty spaces to feed the soil.

Summer prune currents, gooseberries and raspberries after fruiting.

Take cuttings from herbs.

Tidy paths, cut crass and clip edges.

Tie cucumbers, peppers and tomatoes to strong canes.

Watch out for slugs and other pests.

September

Time to sow the following seeds:

Carrots	Radish	Spring cabbage
Endives	Rocket	Swiss chard
Lettuce	Spinach	Turnips

You can plant out now:

Onion sets	Rhubarb	Strawberries
Spring cabbage	Bay	

You can harvest this month:

Harvesting begins to change after this month as the sun appears shorter in the sky, but you will still get a great harvest this month.

Beetroot	Kale	Raspberries
Broad beans	Leeks	Red and black currents
Broccoli	Lettuce	Spinach
Carrots	Parsnips	Strawberries
Cauliflower	Peas	Summer Cabbage
Cucumbers	Peppers	Tomatoes
Potatoes	Radishes	

Other notes:

Cut down asparagus fern as it starts to die and mulch the bed thoroughly.

Cut out old raspberry canes and tie up new ones

Deadhead flowers to prolong the growing season

Dry pumpkins in the sun before storing make sure you keep them off the earth or they will rot.

Earth up celery.

Feed leeks and celeriac with an organic fertilizer.

Lift remaining onions and dry them in the sun or glass house (plat the leaves together and hang them)

Time to order your spring bulbs!

Record vegetable successes and failures in order to plan for next year's planting.

Sow green manure such as hardy red clover or vetch or other green manure mixes.

Check the support for your tomatoes and pepper plants.

Turn your compost heap and water if dry.

October

Time to sow the following seeds:

Broad beans   Mangetout peas

You can plant out now:

Onion sets	Cauliflowers	Winter / spring lettuces
Spring cabbage	Rhubarb	Strawberries
Garlic	Blueberries	

You can harvest this month:

Harvesting begins to slow but still plentiful if you have mulched to help keep the warmth in the soil.

Beetroot	Kale	Raspberries
Broad beans	Lettuce	Red and black currents
Broccoli	Peas	Spinach
Carrots	Peppers	Strawberries
Cauliflower	Potatoes	Tomatoes
Cucumbers	Radishes	

Other notes:

Compost all dying plants unless they are diseased (these go into the skip)

Cut back asparagus ferns and Jerusalem artichokes

Dig over all empty areas and cover with a compost manure mix

Draw up soil around stems of brassicas to keep them stable in the winds.

Earth up celery and leeks

Fork in green manures

Lift all remaining potatoes and store them in a dark dry place

Mulch celeriac and parsnips

Plant spring bulbs

Prune blackberries and raspberries

Sweep up leaves, leave them to rot in black bags or cages.

November

Time to sow the following seeds:

Broad beans	Salad leaves	Lettuce
Mangetout peas	Spinach	

You can plant out now:

Onion sets	All currants	Broad beans
Garlic	Blackberries	Peas
Rhubarb	Gooseberries	Strawberries
Blueberries	Raspberries	

You can harvest this month:

Harvesting is now reduced, but still enjoyable with winter selections.

Beetroot	Carrots	Lettuce
Broad beans	Kale	Peas
Broccoli	Parsnips	Radishes
Cauliflower	Jerusalem artichokes	Spinach

Other notes:

If you have planted out another crop of broad beans and or peas make sure you net them completely!

Beware of hungry mice and rats, protect your crops

Clean and tie all bamboo canes and stakes into bundles and store them

Cut down globe artichokes and protect crowns with mulch or straw.

Dig in green manures sown in late summer.

Lift carrots, beetroot and Jerusalem artichokes and store. Parsnips can stay in the ground, simply pull some up as required.

Net wintering brassicas and trim out any yellow leaves.

Prepare a new asparagus bed if you haven't done so already for the spring planting

Keep protecting cauliflower heads from frost by covering them with the outside leaves (just fold them over).

Prune gooseberries and currant bushes.

Remove all finished annuals and vegetable plants.

Sweep up leaves again and put them into a pile to compost down or black bags or cages.

Wood chips are handy to spread along muddy paths if you have them.

December

Time to sow the following seeds:

Rocket

Winter lettuce

You can plant out now:

Rhubarb

All currents

Blackberries

Gooseberries

Raspberries

Broad beans in mild climates

Peas in mild climates

You can harvest this month:

Harvesting begins this month, even if they are small you can begin and then plant again for a continuous crop.

Brussel sprouts

Sprouting Broccoli

Cauliflower

Kale

Parsnips

Winter Lettuce

Radishes

Spinach

Other notes:

Clear any dead plants from your plots

Clean flower pots, seed trays and tools ready for next year

Draw up soil around your brussels sprouts or stake them for support

Order seeds for next year

Prune currant bushes

Remove yellow leaves from salad leaves and brassicas.

Spread well-rotted manure or compost on your plots if you didn't do this last month

Start planning your plots for next year with crop rotation

Tidy sheds/ storage, check they are secure and weatherproof.

About the Author

Born in Adelaide, South Australia, Sue Messruther has written many well-reviewed books, a good mix for adults and children as Sue is a mother of 6 children and currently 6 grandchildren. She loves her allotment and spends many hours weeding, watering and planning next year's crops, even here her humour shines through as her allotment has street signs!

She has created many adult colouring books, journals and organisers these just continue to grow as inspiration guides her onto the next book.

Sue's children's books are a true delight as she composes all of the images around the stories she creates. Her bestselling children's volume sets include the Just For Kids series, Alien Caper Encounters series and the Dogs, Cats & All Other Animals and let's not forget Messruther's stand-alone titles. In reality Sue has over 300 books published in print and kindle combined and this grows dramatically throughout the year and is why she now breaks up her titles and lists just a few which are similar to this title.

Sue enjoys creating & colouring in her Adult Colouring Books & Journals, some of these have space to add extra doodles, others that are simple and then many images that are challenging! So she has created and use her own books, in fact, many of the journals were created because she had a need for them and her colouring books she needed these for the dementia patients she looks after in her full time job.

Messruther has also contributed writings to the books Thorns to be Thankful For and Skill Share both of which became best sellers in the first week of publication.

There are always more books in the creation cycle, for example a new children's series currently in various stages is the Play Time Books, which forthcoming from the author, includes Come Find Me Under The Sea was the first to arrive in this series soon to be followed by Back In Time With Dinosaurs and then It's A Dog's Life. Titles after this are yet to be determined!

Messruther has lived in Cairns, Queensland, Australia and now currently resides in Scarborough, North Yorkshire, England, with her family and Oscar, an Old English Sheep puppy of gigantic proportions, (Digby is a constant thought and fear, and will Oscar grow that big!) Thankfully, his growth has slowed down now so Digby II is safe from reality!

As with everyone, her life and inspirations grow on a daily basis, so the future is looking very creative indeed, if you would like to follow up with new titles you can contact or read about Sue Messruther and what she is up to on her Facebook page https://www.facebook.com/suemessruther.author/ she would love to hear from you and see any colouring in you have done or comments and suggestions.

CHAPTER TWELVE

Other Journals & Organisers

Journals

My Christmas List Journal

Best & Worst Days Pocket Diary

Saying It Pocket Coloring Journal

You know your cat is the center of your life when.

The Collective Useful Diary – Family

Monthly To Do Journal – Dooley Me

Monthly To Do Journal – Whimsical Me

Monthly To Do Journal – My Heart

Monthly To Do Journal – My Blossom

Monthly To Do Journal – Oh My Timber

Monthly To Do Journal – My Trekking

Monthly To Do Journal – Posy Me

Expressing Myself Journal

Awakening my soul family

Awakening my soul yourself

I wish I had said that!

All That I Did - My Year As I Made It

I Did It My Way - My Year As I Made It

As I See It - My Year As I Made It

What I Did - My Year As I Made It

I Did What? - My Year As I Made It

I Achieved - My Year As I Made It

All That I Achieved - My Year As I Made It

I Achieved It My Way - My Year As I Made It

I Did It! - My Year As I Made It

I Said and I Did It - My Year As I Made It

My Progress - My Year As I Made It

My Life - My Year As I Made It

Bit By Bit - My Year As I Made It

Step By Step - My Year As I Made It

One Step at a Time - My Year As I Made It

One Day at a Time - My Year As I Made It

Month by Month - My Year As I Made It

Day by Day - My Year As I Made It

Through The Year - My Year As I Made It

Every Day Is New - My Year As I Made It

I Made It! - My Year As I Made It

Another Year - My Year As I Made It

<u>Organisers</u>

My Organiser - That's Life

My Organiser - I Rule

My Organiser - For The Weekends

My Organiser - Fantasy

My Organiser - Flower power

My Organiser - Puppy love

My Organiser - Perrrrfect Days

Manufactured by Amazon.ca
Bolton, ON

10370438R00070